WHEN TRAGEDY STRIKES
IN JUST ONE NIGHT

ARCI DAVIS

LIZBETH BOOKS PUBLISHING

DEDICATION

I want to honor an extraordinary lady in my life, my mother. Ma, thank you for sticking by my side since day one. You have never left me. I am eternally grateful for your everlasting love and support. Before I left the hospital, you were the first person to tell me to write a book and share my story with the world. Well, I did it, Ma. If it weren't for you telling me to trust God, I would have never found my strength. I can never repay you for everything you have done, but I will continue to pray for your strength. I love you so so much!

In memory of my dear friend, DeLorean "Bean" Williams. Thank you for taking the time out to come from Atlanta, Georgia, to Jackson, Mississippi, to show me different techniques on how to live with a spinal cord injury. I also would like to thank your parents, Mr. and

Mrs. Williams, for showing my mom how to make things easier as a caregiver. You were a great inspiration in my life. Your death impacted me in a way that I can't explain. I will never forget your beautiful soul. May you continue to Rest Peacefully.

Love Arci

ACKNOWLEDGMENTS

I want to thank all of my friends, whom I didn't mention in the book, for the continuous love and support you have shown me throughout this journey. I love you all: Ashley Adams, Gabrielle Thomas, Donald Silas a.k.a 3, Tandi Johnson, Terrell Hudson, LaQuisha Banks a.k.a Slim, Constance Riley, Michelle Atkinson, and Janez Young.

I would also like to thank my doctors, therapists, and CNA's at Methodist Rehabilitation Center and Lakeland University Physicians: Dr. Villacorta, Dr. Odom-Funchess, Ms.Nichole, Ms. Elizabeth, Ms. KK, Mrs. Debbie, Mr. Chris, Ms. Lisa (CNA), Ms.Roxie, Mrs. Brenda, Ms. Janet, Mrs. Pat, Mrs. Suszan, Mrs. Ashley, Mrs. Nancy, Mrs. Sidney, Mrs. Amanda, Mr. Andre(the tech), and Mr. Greg who've fixed my wheelchair on countless occasions.

I would also like to thank the ladies at the Pavillion who have played a vital role throughout this journey:

Mrs.Gloria

Mrs. Andrea

Mrs. Tasha

And a host of others. I want to give a special shout-out to my cousin Chondra. Thank you for all the times you came over to get me out of the house and for having to pick me up physically just to put me inside the truck before I was able to get a wheelchair accessible vehicle.

Lastly, I want to recognize all the beautiful quadriplegics and paraplegics I have met throughout this journey and a special shout-out to Alivia Welch, who I met and we became great friends. Your strength is admirable. Keep striving for greatness. Together we can do it. The best is yet to come. And to those reading, thank you for your support.

TABLE OF CONTENTS

1

I never imagined my life would be like this at the age of twenty-five. I used to be a cool, vibrant chick who was very career-oriented and sociable. In 2013, I had obtained my bachelor's degree in education from Tougaloo College in Jackson, Mississippi, which landed me a teaching position at George Elementary School. I felt like I had accomplished a lot when I received that position, and I really enjoyed teaching my kindergarten class.

Each day after work, I would wind down in my townhome that I shared with one of my cousins. Every afternoon, I had myself a glass of wine to set the mood for the rest of the day. I would then get comfortable in my favorite loungewear and crash on the couch to catch up on one of my favorite TV series. I even called my boo to come chill. My boo and I talked about our future often. We always talked about going further in our careers, traveling the world, and living our best lives. I made plans and thought I had my life all figured out. I had a boo I was crazy about, my career was popping, and my friends were LIT.

Every weekend, I would link up with my girls after a long week of work. We often texted in our group chat—which we named "crew love"—to plan our weekends. Most of our weekends consisted of going to different restaurants to have drinks. We often went to a Mexican restaurant because their drinks were always a two-for-one price. Otherwise, we would order a pitcher of liquor to share between the four of us and have our normal "girl talk!" Of course, we wouldn't vent for too long, because the drinks we ordered would quickly have us feeling just right. The turn-up wouldn't stop there, however; we would link up at one of our houses to "pre-game" and get a little "buzz" before we hit the streets. We often went to a popular bar in town where they played all the good music, where they sold good drinks, and where all the dancing and "twerking" went down. After turned-up nights out, our group chats were LIT the next day, reminiscing on the fun night we had.

I really thought I had it all together. You can't even imagine how quickly that changed for me on October 8, 2016. I remember that day clearly. I woke up at my usual 6:00a.m. wake-up time so I could make it to George Elementary by 7:30. Once at school, I performed my teaching duties as I would any other day. In the midst of grading papers and doing lesson plans, my phone was going off like crazy, with all my girls texting in "crew love." It was a Friday, so we were all were ready to turn-up. Despite all the work I had to get done, I was still down to link up with the crew. Eventually, I stopped replying in the group chat because I wanted to get as much work done as possible before I left work. I had to finish preparing grades for report cards and getting ready for the parent-teacher conference, which was the following Monday. I looked at the clock at around 3:00p.m. and saw that my workday was slowly coming to an end. I was still swamped with trying to get report cards done, so I decided to take them with me to finish over the weekend.

My first stop when I got off work was the mall to find something cute to wear for the night. I went into one of my favorite stores, "Love Culture," and found a cute green-and-black dress that fell off the shoulder, along with some long black boots. I was excited after I bought my outfit because I knew I was about to be cute for the night! My next stop was to the liquor store. I already knew exactly what I was getting when I got there: a famous wine called "Taylor." It had eighteen percent alcohol by volume, and it was one of the strongest wines I had ever tasted.

After leaving the liquor store, I finally arrived at my townhouse. After a long day of work, it felt good being in my own domain. I quickly settled down and poured myself a tall glass of "Taylor." I sat on the couch with my wine in one hand and my phone in the other, searching for some music to jam to while I sipped my wine. The first song that popped up on my playlist was "Run It Up" by this dope artist named Lucci. I quickly tapped the play button because that song was always a vibe! I continued sipping my wine, and after a few sips in, I could feel the "Taylor" slowly giving me a buzz. By the time I finished my glass, I was definitely "Taylored" (LIT). I headed upstairs to my room to take a nap for a few minutes before the turn-up later on, and when I lay down, I instantly dozed off.

Not realizing how tired I was, a few minutes turned into a few hours. When I woke up, I immediately checked my phone and saw that the girls had been texting in "crew love." Two of my girls were already getting dressed while my other homegirl and I were still lagging around in bed. My phone buzzed again, and it was another message from the crew. It was my homegirl who was in bed already saying she no longer wanted to go. A few minutes later, my phone rang and it was a FaceTime call from one of my girls who was already getting dressed.

"Bitch, let me guess," she said. "You ain't going since our other homegirl ain't going."

"Bitch, I'm going," I replied. We were just talking shit like we always did, and I went ahead and got up to get dressed. I had already planned on going with my girls, and besides, I didn't want to be a party pooper. On top of that, I had already bought a cute outfit for the night that I couldn't wait to wear.

By the time I finished getting dressed, the girls had already pulled up to my townhouse. I quickly headed outside and got in the car. My two girls were in the front, so I got in the back. Someone else was sitting in the back as well, a girl who didn't normally go out with us. She had a big bottle of Remy Martin that she was taking shots of before we made it to our destination, and I could tell she was already faded. For the most part, I really didn't pay her any mind.

When we arrived at our destination, I could tell by the parking lot that there was a nice little crowd on the inside. As we were getting out of the car to head towards the bar, we got a text from our home-girl who was still in bed. She told us to wait on her; she was about to pull up. I was happy she changed her mind because it was always LIT when the four of us linked up.

When we made it into the bar, we went straight to the bathroom to check our hair and snap it up like we always do. After we finished in the bathroom, we headed to the bar for our first round of drinks. When we started feeling our drinks and getting a little tipsy, we were ready to dance and turn-up. My girls and I made our way close to the stage and closer to the DJ booth. The girl who rode with us was being a little standoffish. She wasn't dancing with us or anything. Honestly, it was almost like she wasn't even with us. My girls and I continued to dance and enjoy the night. We had a few more rounds of drinks, and then we headed to the parking lot to go to our next destination. We were about to head to the big club in town where the DJ was known to be off the chain. We were tripping out and were in our zone as we left the club.

Before we went to our next destination, we decided to stop at a gas station. My homegirl that met us at the bar earlier trailed us there. When we pulled up at the gas station, I heard a knock on the window.

"Aye, one of y'all wanna ride with me?" asked my homegirl who was riding by herself. I was too LIT to move at that moment.

"I'll ride," said one of my homegirls who had somehow ended up in the backseat with me after we left the bar. She got out and got in the other car while I waited for the other two to come out of the store. When they came out, the girl that rode with us got in on the driver side and the one who was originally driving that night got in on the passenger side.

We began to drive off the parking lot of the gas station and onto the interstate I-55, and within those few seconds, I fell asleep. I was told later that, as we entered the interstate, traffic was at a steady pace due to the in-town festivities. The fair was in town, and people were enjoying the night throughout the town. I guess you can say the city was LIT that night. As we continued on the interstate, the cars ahead of us came to a standstill, and all the cars behind us began to slow down before coming to a complete stop. The girl who was driving our car was still going full speed, apparently not realizing that traffic ahead was coming to a stop, and out of nowhere, BOOM. All you could hear was the sound of glass shattering as she rammed into the back of a white Infiniti. The impact must've been extremely hard because it caused the Infiniti to hit a seventeen-year-old boy who was pulling his car to the side of the road; the boy ended up suffering two broken legs and a ruptured pelvis.

My homegirl who was trailing us saw that everyone was opening their car door to get out, which ensured her that everyone was okay. A few seconds later, however, she noticed that I never opened my car door. She knew at that very moment that something was wrong. As she walked closer to the car, she saw me thrown to the floor of the back-seat in a kneeling position. She pulled and pulled on the door, trying her best to open it, but the door was stuck. She immediately alerted the paramedics who were on the scene for the seventeen-year-old boy that there was another passenger who needed help, and she was stuck in the car.

I could vaguely hear a lot of commotion, yelling, and loud sirens. I was drifting in and out of consciousness and all I could taste was blood. It felt like I was drowning in my own blood while I was waiting to be rescued. I tried my best to move, but I couldn't, and at that moment, I knew it was serious.

The more I tried to open my eyes to snap back into reality, the heavier and weaker they became. As the paramedics removed me from the vehicle and loaded me into the ambulance to transport me to the university hospital, I could hear them talking to me to keep me responsive. Everything was a blur, and the bright light beaming from inside of the ambulance only made it worse. I tried my best to stay calm for as long as I could before telling the paramedic to call my mother, but when they tried to get in contact with her, they couldn't reach her. I immediately started praying. "God, you made me more than a conqueror [Romans 8:37]. No weapon formed against me shall prosper [Isaiah 54:17]." I repeated it over and over until I finally arrived at the hospital. My thoughts were all over the place, but I knew God didn't let me make it that far for that to be the end.

As they unloaded me from the ambulance, it felt like my body had begun to shut down, because I couldn't feel anything. I wasn't fully aware of what was going on at that moment because I was still intoxicated, but I knew my body was in some sort of shock about what had just happened. When I entered the hospital, they rolled me to a room in the intensive care unit. So many things were running through my head. "Am I going to die? Is this reality right now?" Normally, you hear about these things on the news, not realizing that it could happen to you too.

My mom finally arrived at the hospital, and when

she entered the room, I felt a little at ease because she was the face I had been waiting to see. "Mama, I'm sorry, I can't feel my legs," I blurted out.

She immediately kissed my bloody face—I had a huge gash in my head—and said, "Aww, baby, we will get through it."

A few minutes later, my sister, Tink, walked in. Right as she was walking in, the doctor was finally coming around to give my mother my diagnosis. As the doctor was walking up, he asked my mom, "Does she always get this intoxicated?"

My mama looked at him kind of sideways and replied, "She does on the weekends, during her free time when she's off work."

I thought, "Dang, is it a crime for a chick to have a causal drink on the weekends after a long week of work?"

After the way my mama looked at him and the response she gave him, he knew to go ahead and tell my mama the diagnosis. I overheard him telling my mama and my sister that I had suffered a broken neck and that I was going to be paralyzed from the chest down. He continued explaining, "When a patient breaks their neck at the cervical level, which is connected to the spine, we call it a spinal cord injury." As he went through the diagnosis with my mama, it became apparent that not only was I paralyzed, but I also had a cut on my kidney and liver and a partially collapsed lung.

Before I knew it, I shouted frantically, "The devil

is a liar." In my mind, I was thinking that I was going to have surgery and walk out of the hospital in a couple of days. I didn't realize there was a long road ahead of me and that this was only the beginning!

After the doctor was finished, my mama and sister walked back to the bed where I was lying. I was in a daze, just staring towards the ceiling. Mama looked at me and said, "Arci, I know you're drunk, but are you high too?"

I looked at her and my sister and said, "Y'all, I'm still fucked up!" They could do nothing but shake their heads and laugh.

While waiting in the intensive care unit, a few more people came back to see me. My favorite cousin, Shea, who was my roommate at the time, was one of the faces I remember seeing that night. Shea was always positive and was always cracking jokes, but at this particular time, I noticed she was at a loss for words. We grew up together as babies, so I could look in her eyes and tell she felt some type of awful to see me in that condition. The first thing I said to her was, "I know my boo gonna leave me now."

She laughed, and replied, "Don't worry about that right now. You have bigger problems."

After chatting for a while, my cousin began to leave the room, and someone else entered. My face lit up. It was my boo, but I instantly saw all the sadness and hurt in his eyes. He told me he hated seeing me in that condition and not being able to move. He leaned over the bed and gave me a kiss on the forehead, and then he left the room. My adrenaline was still rushing. I didn't know how to feel at that point, and after his visit, I drifted off to sleep.

I finally woke up the next morning, and my adrenaline was slowly easing. I could hear the sound of the IVs dripping from the machine in my room. As I was lying in the hospital bed, I was a little more alert, and I noticed I was wearing a very uncomfortable neck brace that I vaguely remembered having on the day before. The brace had a lot of different tubes running through it connected to several IVs and to a ventilator. I had never imagined that I would be in the hospital hooked to a ventilator that would be doing ninety-five percent of the breathing for me, but there I was. My mind was all over the place, and the diagnosis my doctor had given my mom kept playing over in my head. I really couldn't fathom the fact that I was paralyzed, meaning I had no movement in my body below my chest. As the day progressed, I began to feel every pain that was inflicted on me internally. That pain was so agonizing!

I had a lot of visitors that day, but my most memorable visitor was one of my best friends. Kendrick, who was also like a brother to me, was distraught when he had heard about the accident. When he arrived at the hospital, he saw my mama standing outside the door of my room. All of a sudden I heard a loud voice saying, "Why? Why did this have to happen to my best friend? She doesn't deserve this!" I heard my mama trying to calm him down, but he was hysterical. He calmed down a little as he entered the room, but he was still crying and shaking his head. Before I could even hold a conversation with him, I started feeling faint. I was feeling really weak and dizzy. The machines I was hooked up to started beeping loudly, and the nurses came back in to check on me.

"Please stop with the visitation until we're able to get her numbers back stable," a nurse said to my mother. "She's going into distress."

My blood pressure started dropping tremendously, and my breathing became shallow. My doctor came into the room as well, and he was immediately concerned. "Everything is starting to decline," he told my mama. "We're going to have to rush her to surgery."

I was rushed to surgery that same day, which was originally scheduled for the next day. I'd never had life-threatening surgery prior to the accident, so the thought of it was terrifying. I was incredibly nervous as the nurses began to unhook the machines in my room. When they finished, they rolled me down the hall on the hospital bed. Halfway to the surgery room, I looked to the side of me where my mom and sister were waving and cheering me on, and I whispered, "I love y'all."

Before I knew it, I was in the surgery room and put to sleep. I had no clue what went on during surgery. When I finally woke up, it was the next day, and I was back in intensive care. All I could remember was me going inside the surgery room, so I tried to speak to figure out what was going on. As I attempted to speak, I realized that I couldn't get a single word out of my mouth. I looked down and saw that there was a long tube coming from my mouth that was placed there after surgery. My doctor must've seen the confusion on my face as I began to look around the room. Before I could even look his way, I heard him say, "She's finally alert."

He quickly made his way over to the hospital bed, but before he could get a single word out, I mouthed to him with the most pitiful and painful look on my face, "Please take it out."

He laughed at my response and said, "I wish I could, but I can't right now." He began to explain, "Miss Davis, your surgery lasted about an hour, and we had to insert a tube in your throat called a throat trachea. The trachea was placed there to help convey air to and from your lungs since your breathing was impaired due to your partially collapsed lung."

I've always heard people say, "When it rains, it pours." I guess that was true, because that's exactly what it felt like in that moment.

He continued, "We had to take a bone out of your hip and place it in your neck along with a couple of screws." He explained what was done to me during surgery, and when he had finished, he left the room.

Once the doctor had left, my mama quickly

grabbed a hand mirror to show me the trachea that was placed in my throat, which was right beside the huge gash on my neck where I had surgery. She then lifted my hospital gown to show me the huge scar on my hip. I immediately felt numb—*physically and mentally*—not because of the scars I received but simply at the thought of what I had to unknowingly endure. "There had been plenty of LIT nights partying with my girls, and we had always made it home safely. Why did tragedy have to strike that particular night?" I thought.

$\sim$

A WHOLE WEEK HAD PASSED, and there I was, still helplessly laid up in the hospital. Every hour, doctors and nurses were coming in and out of my room, monitoring me and doping me up with strong medication to numb the pain. I woke up every day hoping that at any moment I would walk right out of the hospital and continue on with everyday life. My thoughts consumed me most of the time because I was still trying to make sense of that tragic night. "Maybe if I hadn't fallen asleep, I could have braced myself before we crashed," I thought. Every second, my thoughts were on over-drive. That whole week, I was in shock and in disbelief.

After a week of being in ICU, I received a little bit of good news. I was finally being moved out of intensive care into a regular room. I was happy because I was also off the ventilator, which meant I was breathing on my own. I was also able to communicate properly again even though the throat trachea was still there. It had been stressful not being able to communicate, and my jaw had become completely numb from mouthing and spelling out words in order for my nurses and visitors to understand me.

As I lay there still deep in my thoughts, my boo walked through the door. He always seemed to take my mind off the reality of what I had going on, and I was smitten whenever he came around. Normally, he would come during lunchtime so we could eat lunch together. He stayed there with me every other night, which gave my mama a break and time to do stuff for herself. He was also a big help to the nurses who were caring for me. He did anything I asked him to do. I complained a lot about my scalp itching due to some damaged nerves from the accident, so he even bought combs and scratched my scalp for me. It was the little things that mattered. He made me feel so loved, and I knew he was going to be there every step of the way.

I suffered so many injuries from the accident—things I never imagined would have happened to me. Despite everything I had going on physically, emotionally I felt an outpouring of love. I started receiving the sweetest handmade cards from my students and gifts from my principal, coworkers, and friends. My best friends, Keana and Jessika, had to travel miles to see how I was doing and to give me some words of encouragement. I was glad to have their support in the most difficult time of my life. My friend Brittany, whom I met at Keana's wedding, came to sit with me some days as well. She kept me laughing because she was so full of life and positivity, which is what I needed at the moment. I felt so loved but still so numb all at the same time. Everyone went out of their way to show their love and concern for me, and at that point I knew I had to keep fighting.

2

I t was early Saturday morning, and when I looked at the clock, I saw that it was 6:00 on the dot. I was lying in bed, looking straight ahead at the nurses' information board in my room, and the calendar happened to be right beside it. I stared at the calendar for a minute. "Wow," I thought, "it's October 29, 2016, which makes it exactly three weeks since the accident." Lord knows it still felt like it had happened yesterday. I still couldn't get over the fact that I was in the hospital way longer than I expected. And there I was again, with my thoughts on *over-drive!* I closed my eyes, trying my best to doze off before my thoughts got the best of me.

I could vaguely hear someone knocking at the door, but I couldn't tell if it was my imagination or if someone was really at the door. Either way, I didn't bother to open my eyes to see who was there.

Seconds later, I woke up to the sound of my doctor's voice. "Miss Davis, sorry to wake you, but I've got some important news. We've got all your vitals stable enough for you to be discharged."

"Yay, I get to finally go home," I thought.

He continued, "You'll be transported by ambulance to Select Specialty Hospital."

In my head, I was like, "*Really*, doc?"

He went on to say, "Select Specialty is an acute care facility that promotes recovery and is known for weaning spinal cord patients off the throat trachea."

"This is *not* the news I wanted to wake up to," I thought. Even though I was relieved about the fact that I would be getting the trachea removed soon, I was still unhappy because I had to be moved to *another* hospital, rather than being able to go home. I gazed at the ceiling trying to absorb all the information my doctor had given me.

Shortly after, my mom walked in with a big, bright smile on her face while sipping on her coffee as usual. She was right on time because the doctor had just discharged me and the ambulance was arriving soon. My mama quickly gathered my personal items and tossed them into my hospital bag. Next, she took down all the colorful cards my students, coworkers, and friends had sent me that were hanging from the cabinets in my room. She finished packing just as the paramedics were knocking at the door, ready to transfer me from the hospital bed into the paramedic bed. The transfer was so quick and smooth, it was over before I could blink my eyes. They continued to roll me out of my room and into the hallway. As I rode down the hallway while lying on the bed, I felt really . . . strange. I was used to seeing other people being rolled around on hospital beds due to tragic events, but I would have *never* thought I would be the patient. We continued down the hall to the lobby and out of the door where the ambulance awaited. I had to squint my eyes because I hadn't seen the sun shining or been outside in weeks!

Deep thoughts crowded my mind as we headed to Select Specialty. "I never expected that one day I would wake up and forget what a gentle touch felt like," I thought. "My physical freedom was robbed in a matter of seconds." I didn't know if I would ever get over that tragic night. The more I tried to think positively, the more negative my thoughts became.

Looking out the back window of the ambulance, I saw that we had finally arrived at Select Specialty Hospital. When they were ready to unload me, they opened the double doors in the back and rolled me down the ramp onto the bumpy pavement. While they were rolling me up to the door of the hospital, I couldn't help but stare off into the sky. It was such a beautiful day. It was fall, so the breeze in the atmosphere was just right. "Man, it's the perfect day to be out riding, vibing, and enjoying all of life's opportunities," I thought, "but here I am, stuck and confined to a hospital bed." I was still so young and there were so many things in life I hadn't had a chance to experience, so being in that condition was devastating.

When I entered the building, they rolled me towards the nurses' station while I waited for them to prepare my room. The nurses and therapists were all welcoming, and the environment was very pleasant, but that still didn't change the fact that I wanted to go home and back to my comfort zone!

After settling in that day, sleep was the only thing on my mind, mostly because of all the transporting. It was hard trying to catch a nap while the nurses were in and out of my room making sure I had all my meds for the day. It took about thirty minutes before the meds kicked in, and when they did, I was out like a light.

It felt like I hadn't slept in days, but when I woke up, it was only midnight. I tried closing my eyes again, hoping that at any moment I would drift back off to sleep, but I was completely restless! Sleeping was my way of escaping from reality, so I was frustrated at my lack of sleep. I lay there motionless, trying my best to adjust to sleeping in one spot *all night long!* On top of that, I had to do it with a neck brace on! I missed my bed so much that I even had flashbacks of when I was able to crawl in bed and get comfortable with the cool air blowing on my face until I fell asleep. Now things were different, and it was hopeless trying to fall back asleep after the meds wore off. I became very agitated while lying there, so

I counted the tiles forwards and backwards on the ceiling of my room. Every few seconds, my eyes wandered from the ceiling to the clock, watching every minute slowly pass by. I was out of my mind at that point. Daylight was slowly peeking through the blinds when I finally felt myself drifting off to sleep after a long night of torment. It was the same repetitive routine every day and night. The days seemed long and the nights even longer.

I HAD my throat trachea removed successfully after a long week of treatment at Select Specialty. It was such a relief, which meant I was one step closer to going home. That morning after the trachea was removed, I was back on my normal schedule. The nurses came in at around 6:30 that morning to give me my morning meds. I was always moody around that time, as that was the time I normally fell asleep after being sleep-deprived during the night. As my nurse was preparing my medication, I looked at her very nonchalantly and said, "Don't give me any more medication, because I'm healed in Jesus' name." She laughed when I told her that because that wasn't the usual response a patient would give their nurse. But I wasn't a typical patient; I was different. I went ahead and prepared myself to take the meds. I literally cringed on the inside because I absolutely hated taking medication. Most of the pills were bitter and nasty to the taste. And, oh gosh, the really big ones were always hard to swallow. I choked every time no matter how much water I drunk.

My hospital room was like a revolving door. Shortly after the nurse left, the therapists came right on in. When they entered the room, I could feel their energy. I could see that they were eager to work with me. Their energy was so contagious that I was just as eager to work with them as they were with me. They brought so much life into the room. Even though I wasn't able to do therapy in the gym because I was still bedridden, we made things work and did therapy in the bed. I couldn't lift my arms or legs at the time, so I knew therapy was going to be a difficult task.

As they set things up, I continued to lie there and wait for them. When everything was finally set up, one of the therapists said, "Arci, you ready?" I nodded my head and she continued. "I want you to try something. Just close your eyes and imagine yourself moving your arms." I closed my eyes as requested and imagined myself punching the thin air. The feeling was intense; the more I used my imagination, the more intense it felt. I could feel my muscles responding on the inside, and at that moment, I began to have hope. We tried a few more times, and I was excited each time. Although I couldn't move like I wanted to, I was still very hopeful.

After my therapy session was finished, the day

continued to progress and I had a few more visitors. My auntie KaKa, Linda, TT, and my pastor by the name of Pastor Hooks, who had known me since I was a child, came to pray and encourage me. I felt empowered after prayer, and I was hoping that feeling wouldn't go away.

The days were slowly passing by at Select Specialty, and each day my faith grew more and more as I continued to work with the therapists. When I first entered Select Specialty, all I could do was shrug my shoulders, but as time progressed, I regained function back into my arms. I was very impressed with my progress in such little time. God was so faithful to me in that time. I remember when I had first got injured, the doctors had told my mom that I may never regain arm function since my injury was at a high level, but God showed me otherwise. God sent the right two therapists on my path to help me keep hope alive. Unfortunately, my two weeks at Select Specialty were coming to an end, and I was getting ready to move to another facility called Methodist Rehabilitation Center. Even though I had only spent a short amount of time at Select Specialty, I left there on a high note.

～

MY FIRST DAY at Methodist Rehabilitation Center was a Sunday. I only had a day to mentally prepare for the upcoming days ahead, but I was already feeling a little overwhelmed. It was frustrating moving from different places every two to three weeks, which meant I had to get familiar with the facility itself and get used to having new nurses and therapists all over again. While settling into my new facility, I realized that I'd barely heard from my boo. We had spent every day and every night together prior to the accident, so it felt like we were drifting apart. Everything had happened so fast for the both of us, and I think everything started becoming too overwhelming. He had a lot of issues of his own he was dealing with. While we were dating, I found out that he was only separated at the time, not divorced. I know I should have broken things off when I found out, but I didn't because we were already in so deep and I really had hope for our future. Now that I had way more important issues to deal with, I tried my best not to dwell on the situation, even though it was hard for me.

The week at the new facility had officially started, and I was all settled in. It was a big week for me because it was also my first week of therapy in the actual gym. Everything at Methodist Rehabilitation Center was structured and routine. I didn't know how I was going to get in the swing of things since my sleeping pattern was all over the place. Every morning, the nurses came in at around 7:00 to give me my morning meds, feed me breakfast, and get me dressed, since I wasn't able to do any of that myself.

My mind always seemed to be all over the place in the midst of them getting me prepared for therapy. It was crazy how one night had changed everything. Most days it felt like I was living in a dream! Imagine finally getting your life on track, living independently most of your early twenties, and then suddenly *tragedy strikes*, and you're not able to do anything for yourself. It was a total nightmare. Most of the time, I was there physically but my mind was in another world. It was quite burdensome having to rely on total strangers all the time. I never imagined that a night out with my girls would lead to all this. I couldn't even bear the thought of it.

On the very first day of therapy, I remember lying there in bed waiting for the nurses to finish so I could make it to therapy by 8:00. But then I thought, "How was I going to get there since I couldn't walk?" A few minutes later, I saw one of the nurses coming through the door pushing a manual wheelchair. My face suddenly dropped, because it *never* crossed my mind that I was going to be in a wheelchair. That day, reality slapped me in the face once again. In that moment, I had no choice but to accept my fate. It wasn't like I had an option, since that was my only way to get around. I instantly snapped out of it and headed to the sixth floor (the Spinal Cord Gym) with my nurse pushing me in the wheelchair.

When I entered the gym, everything became blurry. My mood changed quickly, and I became very angry. My emotions took over as I thought about all the things I would be doing if I wasn't in rehab, like teaching my kindergarten class, chilling with my friends, and so much more. I tried hard to fight the tears as I saw my physical and occupational therapist headed over to greet me. I was a bit rude when they made it to me because reality had started to hit hard after seeing all the other people in wheelchairs. It was like another world inside rehab; you had older people and a handful of young people in there working hard just to live somewhat of a normal life again. It wasn't the norm for me, so it was extremely hard trying to adapt. My therapists would ask me questions, and I would respond in a very nonchalant way. Honestly, I didn't want to be bothered. I was still trying to cope with things at that point, so rehab seemed overwhelming. I knew I needed their help, though, and I had to cooperate if I wanted to get better.

My occupational therapist continued to show me around the gym. She showed me the different objects and devices we would use. Some of the things she showed me I had never seen nor heard of, let alone thought I would be using at the prime of my life. She briefly went over some things and was immediately ready to work. She started off teaching me some basic arm exercises. It wasn't hard to grasp the concept of what she was doing, but what was difficult was the fact that I would be doing it with limited arm function. I had to lift each arm up and down as high as possible, with three sets of ten. I sat there and tried my best to lift them as high as possible with each attempt. It wasn't so bad once I warmed up, but I was definitely tired when I made it to the third set.

After the warmup routine, we moved on to something a little more challenging. This time she placed each one of my arms on a harness and strapped them to a weight bar. I was instructed to pull down and back up for another three sets of ten. I did what was instructed, but as I was lifting them, it felt like they weighed a ton. And let me tell you, it was the hardest thing to fight through with tears in my eyes. My arms were still so weak at the time that even the slightest movement felt impossible.

Occupational therapy lasted an hour, and once it was done, I had to immediately prepare myself for physical therapy. My physical therapist was already on the gym mat waiting for me so we could get started. He quickly transferred me from the wheelchair to the mat. As I lay there waiting on him to instruct me what to do, my mind was on a million things in a matter of five minutes, not knowing what to expect for this next session of therapy. Then I heard him say, "Arci, we're going to practice sitting up on the mat. Try to hold your balance as much as you can, and I will assist you with the rest."

"Okay, I got this," I thought. "How hard can this be?"

He helped me to a sitting position and leaned me forwards, gently holding my shoulders while I concentrated on keeping my balance. It was only a minute in before I fell backwards on the mat. Little did I know it was way harder than it seemed, and I became very discouraged. The simplest task that I once knew how to do was the most challenging. At that moment, everything felt like baby stages all over again. We practiced a few more times until it was lunchtime. We quickly wrapped up our session so I could prepare for lunch, and I headed back upstairs to my room with my nurse pushing me in the wheelchair.

Shortly after I was back in my room, there was a knock at my door. It was my occupational therapist all prepared to assist me with my lunch. Lunch time definitely wasn't normal for me anymore, since I didn't have any hand function. Not having any hand function made things *extremely* difficult. I wasn't able to grip a spoon or fork, nor was I able to pick up anything. Due to my paralysis, I had lost the ability to open and close my hands. Anything that was placed in my hands would fall to the floor. My therapist tried a few objects on my hand to help me grip the utensils to eat with. It was kind of time-consuming, especially since I was used to diving into my plate and eating at my own pace. After I was all strapped up with the object in my hand, I made my first attempt to feed myself. As I moved my hand from my plate to my mouth, I could feel every muscle straining in my arm. On my first attempt, I made a complete mess like a two-year-old toddler learning how to feed themselves properly for the first time. My feelings were hurt and my pride was crushed, all because I was an adult who had to rely on another adult to assist me with my lunch. I never realized the importance of completing a simple task like feeding myself until I wasn't able to do it anymore.

My first week of therapy felt like trial and error. I was still trying to adjust to my new schedule. Lord knows I wanted to stop, reset, and try again the following week, but I knew that I had to keep pushing. So that's what I intended to do, because I really had hopes of getting back on my feet. In the meantime, the weekend was about to roll around, and I was happy because those were the days I didn't have therapy. I needed those two days to prepare my mind for the week ahead.

The following week was going to be a little different than the previous week. I was receiving a new wheelchair that I had to learn how to operate and drive on my own. It seemed so unreal that I was in a wheelchair. For some reason, it still didn't sit well with me. That whole weekend, I stayed in bed looking at different inspirational stories on YouTube. I ran across this one particular video of a girl from Texas who was also injured in a car wreck. She had suffered a broken neck, which left her paralyzed from the chest down. When she went to rehab, she had some really intense training using different machines and devices, and within months she was back on her feet. I was amazed as I watched her story, seeing her progress in such little time. She really inspired me because it gave me hope that anything was possible.

Before I knew it, the clock hit 6:00 a.m. and it was officially Monday again. Mondays always seemed like the longest day of the week, especially after a two-day weekend, and I knew that today was going to be an especially long day. I was going to learn how to drive a motorized wheelchair, and I wasn't ready. I was dreading having to even get the day started. My nurses came around the normal time they would any other day. They quickly got me dressed and transferred me in my manual wheelchair down to therapy.

When I entered the gym, my physical therapist was already set up and waiting for me to join. Before I made it to him, I noticed the motorized wheelchair from afar. The bright yellow color was what stood out the most. As I got closer, I noticed how big and bulky it was, and it looked like it weighed a ton. When I finally made it all the way over to it, my therapist introduced me to the wheelchair and immediately went over some basic concepts on how to operate it. My mind was in a daze as he was explaining everything. I wasn't the least bit interested in learning how to drive a freaking wheelchair. "It's not like I'm getting a license for driving this thing anyway," I thought. "The only thing I have ever been interested in driving and getting a license in was a car back when I was seventeen years old, and I had no idea then that I would be taking wheelchair lessons." I snapped back into reality in time to hear him finish explaining everything, and then he was ready to transfer me to the motorized wheelchair.

After the transfer, it was time for me to make my first attempt to drive. I was instructed to drive around the gym a few times to get a feel of how to operate the chair. When I got in the chair, I drove around the gym really slowly. In the midst of driving, I was really trying to concentrate on keeping my arm straight and my hand on the joystick without running into anything since my arm balance wasn't the best. It was difficult at first because I had to drive with my left hand. I had been right-handed prior to the accident, so I had to get used to driving with my left hand since that was now my stronger side.

After a few times around the gym, I was told to take a brief intermission. When my break was over, I was waiting for the next obstacle. The next obstacle was a little more challenging. My therapist grabbed some different color cones from the gym closet and instructed me to follow him into the hallway. I watched as he set up each cone on the floor. I kinda already had an idea of what I was about to do. "Arci, I want you to drive through each cone without hitting or knocking them over," my therapist said.

"This shouldn't be too bad," I thought. It kinda

reminded me of the relay races I used to participate in at field day in elementary school. I wasn't a very good driver starting off, so I was interested to see how well this would go. As I prepared myself to make my first attempt, I paced myself. I drove really slowly, and I looked down at each cone to make sure I had enough room before going through each one of them. I saw that I was doing a great job pacing myself the closer I got to the finish line. When I finally made it to the end, I looked back and noticed that I had completed that obstacle without knocking any of the cones over. I guess that was pretty good for my first attempt.

My session had finally come to an end after an hour of learning wheelchair mobility, but the day was still quite early, and I had a few more sessions to attend. My next stop was to the seventh floor for respiratory therapy.

Having a partially collapsed lung made respiratory therapy vital. I needed the therapy to help improve the function of my lungs. By the time I entered the room, the therapist was already sitting at the table working with the other patients. As I slowly rolled up to the table, I noticed a small, clear device that I saw the other patients blowing into. When I got to the table, she pulled out an extra device for me. The device started at five hundred, which was the lowest, and went up to two thousand, which was the highest. I was instructed to blow into the device as hard as I could and aim for the highest. When I made my first attempt to blow into the device with all the wind I had in me, it barely moved. My breathing wasn't a hundred percent at the time, which caused me to score a 500. I looked around at the other patient scores, just being curious, and noticed that older people were scoring higher than me. I felt like a complete failure. Things weren't improving as fast as I had expected.

As I was leaving respiratory therapy, I felt a sense of anger and disappointment grow up on me. I had really expected much more out of all my therapies that day. Instead of heading back to my room to prepare for lunch, I decided to stop by the lobby. The lobby was always quiet and peaceful, and the big window view made for a calming atmosphere. As I waited for time to pass, I played some meditation sounds on my phone, hoping that it would give me a sense of peace. As I sat there in deep thought, I prayed that I would have more successful days with the remaining weeks I had left, because I absolutely hated unsuccessful days at therapy.

During my third week at Methodist Rehabilitation Center, things started becoming more repetitive, especially once I finally got into a routine of everything. In the midst of my therapy sessions that week, I met a guy named Benard. He was one of the nicest and sweetest guys I met while being hospitalized. Since I had a lot going on at the time, Benard was kind of a distraction. It was almost like he was heaven-sent, and he became a great friend. My mom was still working at the time, so most mornings she wasn't able to be there. Before she would leave for work, she made sure to tell Benard to check in on me and make sure I was okay. I appreciated him for all his kind gestures.

Most days after therapy, I would meet Benard in the lobby by the big window. We would sit there for hours just vibing to some music and talking about life's problems. Some days I would even go sit outside with him and wait while he had a smoke. Normally, we wouldn't stay out too long because he had to go check in on his friend who was also in therapy at the time. As for me, I would go back to my room and chill most days.

That entire week, time was passing by quickly, and I still wasn't where I wanted to be on my journey. I also realized that Thanksgiving was right around the corner. It felt really strange, because I was used to the traditional way of celebrating Thanksgiving at home with family. But now things were completely different. I was about to spend my first Thanksgiving in the hospital, and my first Thanksgiving without my daddy. My emotions were all over the place. My daddy had passed on December 21, 2015, the week of Christmas, from a massive heart attack. You can't imagine how hard it was for me to lose a parent as a young adult, and it was even harder for my mom. We both needed him at the time, especially since I had been injured.

～

WHEN THANKSGIVING DAY FINALLY ARRIVED, and despite everything I had going on, it was a blessing to have my mama right there by my side. I knew she was going to make the best of the day for the both of us. My nurses came around like they would any other day to get me dressed and in the wheelchair, even though I didn't have therapy that day. When they finished getting me dressed, my mama was ready to head outside. We were both tired of the gloominess inside the hospital.

When we made it outside, it was like a breath of fresh air. The weather was pleasant and the sun was beaming just right. My mama took a seat on the bench while I drove my powered wheelchair up and down the pavement. Despite enjoying the fresh air, it was still a boring nontraditional day for us. Shortly after, my sister, Tink, and my brother-in-law, Mike, pulled into the parking lot with my niece and three nephews. I was so happy and relieved to see them. They walked up and took a seat right beside my mama on the bench. We sat out there reminiscing on old times, and we cried laughing at ourselves. We enjoyed sitting out there for a long time before we decided to head back inside.

We headed upstairs to my room, and we tried to make the best of the day by watching holiday movies together. I reclined my powered wheelchair in an effort to get comfortable, and before I knew it, I drifted off to sleep in the wheelchair. My mama woke me up shortly after I dozed off, telling me to come to the lobby with her to get some coffee. I thought it was quite strange, because normally she would go get coffee without me, especially when I was asleep. We headed out the door down to the lobby, but before I could even enter the lobby, all I heard was "SURPRISE!" It was my family. My aunties, cousins, and uncle were all there. I was both shocked and happy to see them all at once. Everything was nicely decorated, and the food looked amazing. The principal who I had been working for prior to the accident even had food from Piccadilly catered. I was very pleased that my family went out of their way to bring Thanksgiving to me. As soon as I got a whiff of the delicious food, I was ready to dig in.

For a moment, it slipped my mind that I couldn't dig in like I wanted to. My sister, Tink, fixed me a full plate and sat down beside me to feed me since I hadn't mastered feeding myself at the time. My heart was full of joy as I ate with my family. When everyone was done eating, they decided to have a little fun by doing this well-known social media challenge called the mannequin challenge. Each person had to strike a pose without moving while the music was playing. Unfortunately, I wasn't able to participate, so I sat there and enjoyed watching them until they finished. When they finished, everyone started cleaning up and getting ready to wind the night down. Overall, my Thanksgiving turned out to be quite joyful with the love from my family. My first holiday spent at the hospital was definitely one to remember.

Finally, it was my last week of therapy in the hospital. I was excited to be going home, but I was also emotionally disappointed. I had really expected to be walking before my release day. In my mind, I was still that same strong girl before my injury, not really realizing that my injury was severe and that it was going to take way longer than the short amount of time I spent in the hospital to get me where I desired to be. I tried my best to look on the bright side of things that week. Despite everything I was feeling, I noticed that the basic things I had worked on at each session that week had improved from the previous weeks. I was able to sit up longer than a minute at physical therapy. I was able to feed myself a little better with the assistive device, and my scores at respiratory increased from five hundred to seven hundred.

In the midst of everything, since it was my last week, I wanted to leave while feeling somewhat normal again. I quickly made arrangements to get my nails and hair done, because I refused to look like what I had been through. So, on the day before my release day, I called my cousin Chondra to see if her nail tech had any vacant spots. Luckily, she did, and she was able to accommodate my needs in the hospital. It felt so good being able to get pampered again. Shortly after that, I called my cousin Shea—since she was always one phone call away—to come style my hair nicely for me. She really knew my style, so she hooked me up with a side-part blonde bob. I loved rocking blonde hair since it accented my skin tone so well. I was really feeling myself when she finished, and on top of it all, my mama had my outfit ready for the next day.

December 7, 2016, was the day I had been awaiting for a long two months. It was the day that I was finally being discharged from the hospital. The clock had just hit 7:00a.m., and my mama was already up and dressed, excited that it was our last day. I was excited to be going home, and even more excited that I finally had a chance to put some regular clothes on other than hospital gear. I've always heard the saying, "When you look good you feel good," and that's exactly how I planned on feeling despite the circumstances.

My nurses came to my room around 8:00a.m. that day to get me dressed in the outfit my mama had laid out. They dressed me in a burgundy dress that fell off my shoulders, a fur vest, and my long black boots. When they finished getting me dressed, I rolled by the mirror in my room to see how everything turned out. I definitely looked like myself; the only difference was that I was still in a wheelchair. My mama and I continued to wait in my room until my sister, Tink, my brother-in-law, Mike, and the kids got there. When they arrived, my sister took pictures of me before we headed up to the Spinal

Cord Gym to say goodbye to some of my favorite nurses and therapists.

When I entered the gym, everyone's faces lit up because they were totally shocked to see me in regular clothes. "Wow, look at you," one of my therapists said. "I've never had a spinal-cord-injury patient released with six-inch heels on." Before we said our good-byes, my sister snapped some pictures of me with my therapists so that I would always hold on to the memories. At that moment, it was bittersweet.

Before I left, I made sure to say goodbye to my friend Benard. When I arrived on the third floor, I could see him already standing outside my room. As I rolled up, I could see that he was a little sad that I was leaving, and so was I. We had built a great friendship in such little time. We snapped a few pictures and exchanged numbers so that we could always keep in touch. After saying goodbye to Benard, my family and I headed to the first floor to finally depart from the hospital. Before we headed out the door, my mama stopped and stared me in the eyes. "We are about to enter into another phase of this journey," she said. "Are you ready?" I stared back at her, speechless.

3

I waited out front of the hospital under the patient loading shed while my mama loaded the car. For some reason, I was still pondering that question she had asked me before we headed out the door. "Maybe I'm still living in a dream and haven't fully woken up from that tragic night," I thought. I really didn't know what to expect now that I was finally discharged from the hospital. I was still deep in thought when the roaring sound of car pipes startled me. It was my mama finally pulling around under the shed. When she pulled up, I noticed that she was in the car I had purchased prior to the accident. It was a silver Chevy Camaro with racing rims, which had always been one of my dream cars. Ever since I had been old enough to drive, I had a thing for a low-riding sports car. I loved hearing the sound of the pipes every time I cranked it up. I took pride in driving my car because it was something I had purchased on my own without the help of my parents.

When my mama got out to transport me from my wheelchair into my car, it felt weird being in the passenger seat of the car that I was so used to driving myself. Anxiety overcame me within a matter of seconds as I realized it was my first car ride since the accident. I knew mama would take her time driving with me on the passenger side, so I tried to relax, but as soon as I felt my back on the seat, I went into a daze. All I could think about was the last time I had driven my car. I instantly started thinking about the times when I used to low ride through the city with my shades on or hit the interstate while bumping my music. I had a whole playlist of all my favorite songs. My music always had me in a zone while jamming through town as if I was the coolest person on the road. I was definitely going to miss riding solo through the city to clear my head after a long day. Unfortunately, I realized that it would be a while before I got behind the wheel again. The only thing that I would be driving was my powered wheelchair at the moment.

My thoughts continued to race as my mom drove through town. I wasn't even paying attention to where we were going, but I snapped back to reality when we came to a complete stop. I saw that we had arrived at our destination: the townhouse I had lived in prior to the accident. Lord knows I wanted to go inside and dive into my king-sized bed again. But things weren't that simple anymore. My mama went inside to collect a few personal items while I waited in the car.

When she came back to the car, we headed to my aunt KaKa's apartment, which was going to be our new home for the time being. Mama was in the process of getting us a new home that was wheelchair accessible. My townhouse wasn't an option since my bedroom and the bathroom were both located upstairs. My aunt's place was already wheelchair accessible, so it was easier to maneuver there until the realtor got back with mama. It was hard to accept the fact that I wasn't able to live on my own again—independently. I had no other choice but to move out of my townhouse, but I had created so many memories while I was living there that it was heartbreaking to have to leave my comfort zone and move so suddenly. I didn't know how I was going to adapt being at my aunt's place, because all I could think of was that there was no place like home. When we arrived at my aunt's place, my sister, brother-in-law, and the kids were already there. When my mama rolled me through the door, I noticed the table decorated with balloons, party food, and a cake that said, *Welcome Home, Arci*. I could really feel the love, and it was special being surrounded by my family.

Before we cut the cake, I called Kendrick—who I referred to as my brother—to come chill and eat with me since I was finally home from the hospital.

When he arrived, I was happy to see him outside of the hospital, but I could tell in his eyes that he hated seeing me in my condition. I had always been so hyperactive around him, so seeing me in a wheelchair with a neck brace and arm splints on was hard for him. Despite the circumstances, we sat there and reminisced on the old times. We had created so many funny memories that we talked and laughed for the longest time at all the dumb stuff we did back in the day. In that moment, I would have given up anything to get those times back. It made me think that you never really realize the importance of a special memory that you share with someone until something tragic happens and you aren't able to do the things you used to do.

A few hours had passed and we were still sitting there enjoying the memories. I was happy to be in the presence of one of my peers again. After the accident, I had started feeling emotionally detached from everything and everyone. I didn't know how to remain sociable and deal with everything I had going on, and a part of me had felt like my peers weren't going to understand how to accept me with the condition that I was in. Hanging with Kendrick gave me hope that I'd still have some of those relationships.

The night was winding down and it was time for my mama to get me ready for bed. Getting ready for bed was totally different now. Everything was based around my mama's time, because she was fully my caregiver. It was an uneasy feeling having to be on someone else's time when I was so used to being on my own time, especially when putting myself in bed. And there I was, feeling like a child all over again.

After a restless sleep, I woke to see that the sun had risen again, as it did every morning. It was officially day two since I'd been out of the hospital, but all the excitement I had about being home had completely faded away. I found myself sinking more and more into depression. Not being able to get around like I used to was starting to get the best of me. I missed the simple things in life, like waking up and getting out of bed at my own pace or getting that morning stretch after a good night of rest. Now I lay in bed and relied on someone else to get me up, and that itself was quite stressful. I now relied on routine, and I missed the spontaneous side of me. Since I was a teenager, I had always craved nightlife fun, and I had enjoyed going on spontaneous adventures with my friends on the weekends. I missed the times when I would randomly go out of town just to get away.

The more that I sat in my auntie's apartment doing nothing, the more disconnected I became from the world and disconnected from the person that I had become. My whole world became dark, and I was screaming on the inside to get out. I was still in my prime, and I wanted to live my best life. Instead, it felt like the life I once knew had been ripped from me in just one night, and although I was still breathing, I felt dead on the inside. I was trapped in my own body and mind, and I wanted to be free again physically and mentally.

The days were going by slowly but surely, and it was time for me to get back into the groove of things, like going back to physical therapy. It had only been five days since I had been out, but it felt way longer. Mentally, I wasn't prepared to go back so soon. Out of those five days, I spent most of my time in bed because I felt like there was no point in getting up. Physically, I knew that my body really needed the training, but my mind thought otherwise. Most of the time my mama could feel the negative energy I let off. "Arci," she told me, "just because things aren't happening like you want them to doesn't mean it's not gonna happen. Baby, everything is on God's timing." I was stubborn, and I didn't want to hear what she was telling me. My human nature wanted the quick fix right then and there. I wasn't ready to face the trials of this journey up ahead. I had already suffered long enough.

4

On December 12, 2016, I was scheduled to go back to Methodist Rehabilitation Center. When the clock hit 6:00a.m., my day official started, and out the corner of my eye, I saw daylight peeking through the blinds. I dreaded my morning routines, mainly because my nights were never easy. I had only gotten a chance to close my eyes for maybe two hours, which felt like only a thirty-minute nap. I was *beat*. But my mama was quite the caregiver. She was getting me dressed all while preparing breakfast so I could make it to therapy by 8:00.

Within an hour, I was in my powered wheelchair headed to the table so I could eat breakfast. When I rolled up to the table, my aunt KaKa strapped my splint to my hand so I could feed myself while my mama was in the back getting dressed. My appetite wasn't the best at the time because there were a million and one things on my mind, but I somehow still managed to get most of it down. When I had finished breakfast, we were pressed for time, so we quickly headed outside so they could transport me from the wheelchair into the car. I rolled up to the door of the car as close as I could get, and my mama then grabbed my upper body while my aunt grabbed my legs. Within a few minutes, I was in the car on the way to therapy with thirty minutes left to spare. During the entire ride to therapy, I listened to my mama as she gave me positive pep talks, but mentally I still wasn't feeling it.

When we finally pulled into the parking lot at outpatient therapy, I suddenly had a heaviness overcome my body. It still felt really strange entering new places that I never imagined would be taking place in my life. By the time my mama had transported me from the car into the wheelchair, a thousand things had run across my mind. "I wonder what therapy is going to be like at this new facility," I thought. "Looking at different inspirational stories of people with spinal cord injuries on YouTube in other states got me feeling like this is my chance to beat the odds. But here I am again, overthinking, trying to conquer this traumatic injury in my mind only to get let down again by my body. How much longer am I going to have to wait for this body of mine to act right?"

My mama rolled me towards the door and into the building. After we signed in at the desk, we waited out in the lobby to get called back to the gym by whatever therapist I would be working with. As we waited, I anticipated getting the day started while still not knowing what to expect for the first day. Moments later, I was greeted by my occupational therapist, who asked us to follow her inside the gym to a designated mat. As my mama rolled me towards the mat, I noticed some of the same equipment that I had used in my previous facility. Before we got started, she informed me that the first day was only for an evaluation. All the anticipation that I had in the lobby had completely gone away once I knew what to expect.

The therapist started off by testing my motor skills to see how much core strength I had, how much mobility I had in my arms, and how strong my muscles were. During the entire evaluation, I was thinking, "Lord, I need a miracle because I'm really weak. I can barely do half of the things she's looking to see if I can do." It was so hard trying to disguise my feelings at therapy. She finished up the evaluation, and shortly after, I met my physical therapist, Megan, who I was going to work with for the time being.

Megan was sweet right from the time I met her. She was gentle and patient with me, and I really enjoyed conversing with her about my injury. She was the first person besides Kendrick that I had actually held a real conversation with since being discharged from the hospital. She quickly transferred me from the wheelchair onto the mat so we could go ahead and start the evaluation. The first part of the evaluation was something called a pin test. The pin test was performed with a safety pin, which meant she had to stick the pin on certain parts of my body to see how much feeling I had below my level of injury. "I've never seen or heard of a test being done like this," I thought, "but everything is all so new to me that I never know what to expect."

While she was sticking the pin on certain areas of my body, I had to let her know if I could feel it. I lay there on the mat with my head tilted back towards the ceiling, really trying to imagine myself being able to feel the pin by taking guesses, but in all honesty, I felt nothing. Thirty minutes to an hour passed by, and the evaluation was over. I was officially done for the first day.

Before we got ready to exit the building, we stopped by the front desk to get my schedule for the rest of the week. As we were headed out the door on the way to the car, my mama was reading my schedule to me, informing me that Monday, Wednesday, and Friday were my assigned days. As she was talking, my mind drifted off somewhere else. By the time we finally got in the car and were headed back to my aunt's house, I was wearing my heart on my sleeve. The feeling of despair was staring me in the eyes. All my life I'd heard my parents tell me to never give up or lose hope, but at this particular point in my life, it was a struggle to keep hope alive since my body wasn't showing any new signs of life.

When we finally arrived back at my aunt's place, I headed straight to the back so my mama could put me in bed. I wasn't in the mood for anything. It was only noon, so I still had a full day ahead of me, but sleeping was my only escape from reality.

Over the next couple of weeks, I continued to attend therapy, but my progress was still at a slow pace. On December 21, 2016, I was scheduled to have my first official doctor's appointment since being discharged from the hospital. It was a cold Wednesday morning, but I was excited because it was the day that I was possibly going to have my neck brace removed by the neurosurgeon who had performed my neck surgery.

My mama and I arrived at my appointment fifteen minutes ahead of time. While we were waiting in the lobby, the thing that stood out to me the most were the patients in wheelchairs, even little kids. It really had me thinking, "What were their reasons for being wheelchair-bound? Had I taken life for granted all these years? I had always been a healthy girl with no health complications, but now I see I'm no different from these patients who have possibly been dealing with disabilities since birth." My thoughts were still wandering when I was startled by a tap on my shoulder from my mama letting me know that the nurse was ready for me. We headed to the back to start the appointment.

When I arrived in the back, the nurse immediately took me inside the X-ray room to take pictures of my neck. Within five to ten minutes, the X-rays were over, and I was sent inside a little room to wait for the doctor to come in and read me the results. I'd been wearing the brace since the night of the accident, so I was eager to have it removed. It was the most uncomfortable feeling ever.

Another thirty minutes had passed before the doctor finally came into the room to read my results. He sat down at the computer and pulled up the fracture of the bones that were repaired during surgery on the screen. "Well, it looks like things are healing well. The bones that we repaired are aligned nicely," the doctor said.

"It's amazing how doctors perform miracles during surgery," I thought. "That is the best news I've gotten since being injured."

He then proceeded to remove the neck brace. As he was removing the brace, I could feel the weight of my head on my neck. I knew it was going to take a while before I got used to not wearing a brace again.

The good news I had gotten from the doctor put my mama in the mood to do a little shopping. Christmas was only a few days away, which had always been one of my favorite holidays, but this time I wasn't in the Christmas spirit. Mama pulled up to one of my favorite stores called *Shoes Forever*. "Arci, would you like to get out and shop with me?" my mama asked. I stared at her blankly with no response, so she went ahead and got out while I waited in the car.

It was always a task getting me in and out of the car, so I wanted to save her and myself the trouble. Besides, I was too embarrassed to be seen in the public eye in a wheelchair. I wasn't ready to risk the chance of being seen by someone I knew. "It felt good when I was able to freely walk in the store and shop for myself," I thought. "I miss those times. Everything was all good just two months ago. Why did my life have to change so suddenly and drastically?" I couldn't understand it.

A few minutes later, I got a FaceTime call from my mama. "Look at the dress and boots I picked out for you. You like it?" she asked.

"Yeah, they're cute," I replied in a low tone. She knew my style so well. Mama did anything to make me smile. I was saddened that I couldn't give her the response that she desired from me. Mentally, it was hard on me trying to pretend everything was okay. Life wasn't normal anymore. My mama came out of the store shortly after our call, and we headed back to my aunt's place to settle in for the rest of the day.

Sunday, December 25, 2016, was a gloomy Christmas morning. The clock had hit 8:00 and mama was in the midst of getting me ready so we could make it to church by 10:00. Mama had already laid out everything the night before, which made things go by a lot smoother and quicker. She dressed me in the outfit she had picked out for me the day we went shopping. I wore a long-sleeved olive-green dress with some long, burgundy peep-toe boots. She finished everything up on me within thirty minutes, and then she proceeded to get herself dressed while I waited up-front for her to finish.

So many things crossed my mind while I waited. "I know God kept me alive for a reason, but I don't understand why my freedom was taken away. At this point, I'm not trying to find out . . . I just want my old life back ASAP." I was still so stuck in the past and how I used to live my life that I couldn't focus on the journey up ahead.

When my mama was finally done getting dressed, we headed out the door. The clock hit 9:55 as we pulled into the church parking lot, with only five minutes left to spare. I heard the melody of "You Are Amazing God" from the outside before we entered the building. It was one of my favorite gospel songs, and the choir was singing it beautifully. As we entered the building, we were greeted at the door by the usher, who also led us to a specific sitting area. The choir was still singing as we were getting situated.

As I sat in my chair, trying to feel the spirit of God by how peaceful the atmosphere was, my mind was roaming all over the place. When the thirty minutes of praise and worship were over, Pastor Sino got up to deliver the message. The more I tried to focus on the message, the harder it was to stay in tune. My mind was simply crowded by too many things. Another hour and a half passed before the service came to an end, but I hadn't gotten a single thing from the message.

Before we were about to head back to the car, my mama stopped by the fountain in the lobby to get me a drink of water. The pastor was in the lobby as well, and we locked eyes just as we were about to head out the door. "Hello, princess," Pastor Sino said in his African accent. I greeted him back with a cheerful heart despite the way I was really feeling. "Don't get discouraged with the way things may seem right now," he told me. "Things change at any given moment if you have the faith to believe that they will. The time will come when you will get married and have beautiful children."

After talking with Pastor Sino, we headed back to the car to head over to my sister's house for the remainder of the day. During the entire car ride, I was pondering over what my pastor had said to me. I had always dreamed of getting married and having kids one day, but now I wasn't so sure. "No man is ever going to accept me in this condition," I thought. The feeling of doubt had set in my mind when I was released from the hospital, but I kept hearing the people closest to me tell me to keep the faith. It was so hard trying to keep the faith when I was facing something so traumatic.

When we arrived at my sister's house, we got inside right as my niece and nephews were opening their gifts. It gave me a little joy to be there in their presence and watch them open gifts. Meanwhile, the smell of fried fish and french fries coming from the kitchen had finally given me somewhat of an appetite. My brother-in-law was quite the gentleman. He fixed everyone a plate, and we all sat amongst each other eating while watching the kids play. They were happy to have mama and me over, and they immediately started planning for the New Year since it was right around the corner. Overall, it was a pretty good day.

On January 1, 2017, officially New Year's Day, I was lying in bed, awakened by the sound of fireworks that went off just after midnight. My bed sat right next to the window, which made the fireworks sound even closer. It wasn't the typical New Year's for me, as I normally brought it in at church and then out celebrating with friends. Now I lay in bed wishing I could be out doing those things just one more time, only this time I would cherish the moment a little longer. I lay there for hours before finally closing my eyes and drifting off to sleep again.

When daylight approached, I kept sleeping, and it was noon before I finally came through. Mama was already dressed for the day. When she saw that I had come through, she proceeded to get me dressed for the day, even though we didn't have any real plans besides sitting in the living room doing absolutely nothing. I hated the way things were, especially considering how I'd always been a spontaneous chick. It drove me nuts to be sitting in the house on a holiday like New Year's.

Later that evening, my sister and her crew pulled up at my aunt's place just like they had planned on Christmas. We all went outside with a glass of wine and sat around watching the kids pop fireworks. While we were all enjoying the fireworks, my mama got a phone call from her personal realtor letting her know that she had finally found us a house to accommodate my needs. I guess that was good news, but nothing was exciting to me anymore, so I didn't know if I was supposed to be happy or what. I just knew I had to move *again* and start over in a new environment. Moving was never fun.

On January 17, 2017, we moved into our new home. I was thankful that this time it was permanent. The house was a nicely sized four-bedroom with two full bathrooms, and there was definitely plenty of room for me to maneuver. Things still felt out of the ordinary, however. Starting over on this journey was always the hardest for me. I missed my townhouse and the ability to take care of myself. My life had been on a roller coaster since October 8, 2016, and the only difference now was that this one was still rolling.

It took my mama and me a while before we got things situated in our new home. We tried to take each day one at a time, even though most days were lonely and boring since I wasn't mobile enough to get around. Those were the times depression sunk in the most. Several of my peers would reach out to me through phone calls, but I was often too wrapped up in my feelings to even pick up. Mama always heard my phone going off and would tell me to answer the phone. She knew I needed the company of my peers to help uplift my spirits. After my mama spoke those words, there were a few times when I did find the courage to pick up the phone and hang with my peers. I would even go to dinner with them, but it was always embarrassing because they would have to feed me. Sometimes I would go riding with them, but it was always a hassle getting me in and out of the car. Being amongst my peers wasn't the same anymore. I couldn't do the things that they could, and I was always traumatized whenever I got in a car. There were times when I completely isolated myself because I was embarrassed about the condition I was in.

I spent a lot of lonely days in my den, surrounded by the TV and the four walls with nothing to look forward to. It was hard being young with no excitement going on in my life. The only thing that even slightly motivated me was going to therapy every other day, wishing that I would receive a miracle at any moment. There were even times when I wasn't thrilled about going to therapy, since my mama was no longer taking me. I missed her motivational talks in the car, which I often needed to start my day.

However, it was a hassle for my mama to get me in and out of the car, so we had to rely on other resources to make her job easier. Now I was getting a ride from a group that provided transportation for people with disabilities. With this transportation, I didn't need anyone to lift me to get in and out. I was able to drive my powered wheelchair into the vehicle with no problems. It was mostly okay, but anxiety always came over me every time a different driver picked me up. After the accident, getting into a vehicle was one of my biggest fears. I always feared that I would have another accident, especially if I wasn't familiar with the person's driving history. I didn't know how I was going to overcome getting used to the different transportation drivers.

Months passed, but I was still faced with many adversities. In the summer of June 2017, I experienced countless sleepless nights. Not being able to sleep at night but finally falling asleep as morning rose had become a trend for me since the accident. I didn't know what normal sleep was anymore. Every time I would attempt to close my eyes, I would wake right back up. It was almost as if I was living life on the edge. Most nights I didn't bother getting in bed at all. I stayed in my chair from sunrise to sunset, mainly because it was easier for me to maneuver in the chair.

Every morning at around 3:00a.m., I found myself in tears until my eyes were puffy and red. My thoughts tormented me by the way my life turned out at the peak of my adulthood. Through all this, not only was I sleep-deprived, but I also deprived my mama of sleep. My crying always startled her from the next room, and she would come to my rescue with the Bible in her hand. She would read different verses so I could find peace to get some rest. After listening to her read those verses, I would recline my chair to get comfortable and would attempt to close my eyes. Staying in the chair was comforting for the moment, but it only made things worse when I started to develop open pressure sores. I knew that I needed to get in bed, but staying in my chair kept me from being confined to the bed with everything I was dealing with. Depression had completely dominated my mind, body, and soul. I had always heard stories of people who had gone through depression, but I never really took thought of it until I fell victim to it.

Like I said before, I was faced with many adversities that physically took over me. In September 2017, my mama prepared a nice dinner for her and me one Sunday evening. She was standing in the kitchen fixing my plate while I was sitting in the dining room contemplating how was I going to eat dinner. I didn't have an appetite, but I also didn't want to let my mama down. Just as she was walking towards me with my plate in her hand, she paused. She could tell by my demeanor that food was the last thing on my mind. "Baby, go look in the mirror. You're losing three pounds a day not eating. You can't just sit here and let yourself waste away. Do you not care about living anymore?" Mama asked in a soft tone.

I drove my powered wheelchair to the hallway to look in the mirror that was mounted on the wall. I saw that depression was really starting to show in my appearance. I rolled back to the dining area where mama was sitting and replied with tears in my eyes, "I really don't care what happens to me anymore. This isn't living to me." Mama was heartbroken by my response, but I couldn't disguise my feelings anymore. From that day forward, I avoided the hall mirror that led to my room, because I couldn't face the reality of what I was becoming.

IN LATE OCTOBER 2017, it was in the middle of the night when out of nowhere I found myself gasping for air. "MAMA, MAMA," I called out while barely able to catch my breath. Mama ran into the room before hysterically calling the paramedics. I lay there trying to remain calm and catch as many breaths as possible. About fifteen minutes later, I could hear the sirens as the paramedics pulled up outside. When they made it inside, they immediately checked my oxygen levels. My levels read eighty-seven, and they were supposed to be between ninety-five and one hundred. The paramedics proceeded to load me onto the ambulance to head to the hospital. On the ride there, I dreaded the fact that I was headed back to the hospital so soon. While in the ambulance, I tried to remain calm, and they placed an oxygen tube in my nostrils to help with the shallow breathing.

When we arrived at the hospital, I was immediately rolled back to intensive care. This brought back memories of the tragic night of the accident. There I was again, laid up in the hospital and back where I started. The doctor came in shortly after I arrived to give me the diagnosis. I listened as he stated, "Miss Davis, you have pneumonia in your lungs, which is the cause for your shortness of breath. Due to your partially collapsed lung, you're more prone to infections." At that point, everything went in one ear and out the other. I was tired of hearing bad news. After spending a few days in the hospital and getting antibiotics through my IV, I was finally discharged.

The rest of 2017 went slowly by, and I reflected on everything I had endured. Throughout the entire year, I had lost hope, I had faced many trials, and I had isolated myself from the world due to embarrassment. Most importantly, I had lost touch with the vibrant young chick I once was.

Now it was 2018, the new year had hit, and yet, I still faced several more setbacks. Staying in my chair 24/7 only made things worse for me. I had previously developed pressure sores by staying in my chair and not getting in bed, and those sores took a turn for the worse. I was referred to a wound care facility that specialized in pressure sores, and they determined that my flesh had begun to eat down to the bone, which became stage four sores. Every two weeks, I had to follow up with the wound care doctor. At one of my visits, the doctor cut me no slack. She strongly enforced me to stay in bed in order for the sores to start healing. Being confined to the bed was the thing I hated the most, but at this point, it was life or death.

For weeks I lay in bed, watching the sun rise every morning and set every afternoon. Life was passing me by every day. I was no longer going to therapy, which only pushed me further away from accomplishing goals. I was miserable just lying there. The only time I really got out was when it was time to follow up with the wound care facility to keep a close eye on my pressure sores. During one of the follow-up visits, my doctor encouraged me to eat plenty of protein to help with the healing process. The problem was that everything I was dealing with had me lacking the most important thing: an appetite. Everything felt difficult when it came to my healing process.

The longer I was on bed rest, the deeper I went in my thoughts. In my head, I could hear my mama's voice saying, "You can't just sit here and let yourself waste away." I realized that, slowly but surely, that's exactly what was happening to me. I pondered it over and over. "Am I really gone give up on life, or am I gone find the strength to pick up the pieces?" My mama did everything she could to help. She even called our pastors, Sino and Suno, to come by the house to give me some words of encouragement. Now it was left up to me, and I knew I had to make some quick decisions.

During the peak of summer 2018, months had passed since I'd been diagnosed with stage four pressure sores. Since then, I had been hospitalized several times for various reasons. At one point, I was starting to think the hospital had become my new home. But, thanks be to God, I made it through those tough times with a new outlook on life. I was still following up with the wound clinic, and although the healing process was slow, I was able to go back to therapy. That summer, I was slowly coming out of depression thanks to the prayers of my family and pastors. I was also thankful for Kayla, who was another one of my best friends. Kayla had been calling me for months, but I would never answer the phone. Those were the times I had completely isolated myself from everyone. But that summer, when I finally came around, she was there to help uplift me when I needed a friend the most. At first, I couldn't see the light at the end of the tunnel, until one day I decided enough was enough.

Where do I begin to tell you how different things are for me now? It took a lot of setbacks and hardships to get the mindset I have now. You've read how I faced tragedy, had to make adjustments, and sank into a deep depression. But I have one question: who wants to face tragedy when things are going right? No one, right? Well, that was me before tragedy struck at the peak of my adulthood. Oftentimes, when you're young and things are going well in life, you hope for every day to be that way. I sure did, but I have since come across a Bible verse that stood out to me. It states in John 16:33 (NLT), "Here on earth you will have many trials and sorrows. But take heart, because I have overcome the world." Sometimes when tragic things happen in life, you never really see the bigger picture that God wants you to see until you've gone through the trials. Well, that was me in the beginning, but through it all, I've developed a better character as a person. Maybe you're wondering, like I did, why we must go through trials to develop a better character. I realized that it helped me build a strong relationship with God so that I can confidently face what life has to offer me on this journey with faith in him. I wasn't ready or equipped for the journey life had given me at the prime of my life, but what I've realized is that a new life can happen at any given moment. A disability doesn't discriminate against anyone, and what I've learned is that I have the choice to pick up the pieces and have faith to keep going or to sit there in sorrow and let life pass me by.

God has a purpose and a plan that is far greater than my own. As I reflect on how things were in the beginning, it brings me to a place of awareness, humility, and priority. Going through a traumatic injury made me more aware of just how precious life really is. I need to be thankful for every single moment, because things can change so fast. Life had a way of humbling me. I'm humble enough to know that you can have it all—health, success, etc.—and lose it all within a blink of an eye. I've always been a church girl, but I kind of kept God on standby. It is now my first priority to consult with God concerning my life instead of trying to figure things out on my own.

As I've grown closer to God, I now realize the true meaning of Jeremiah 29:11, which says, "'For I know the plans I have for you,' says the Lord. 'They are plans for good and not for disaster, to give you a future and a hope.'" Before I got injured, I had many plans for my life, but everything I planned turned out to be the total opposite. This made me realize that God has the beginning and the end of our lives in his hands, and sometimes our own plans don't work out so his plans can be fulfilled. I still don't understand it all, but I continue to trust the process.

When I get discouraged, I'm often reminded of the story of Job in the Bible. Job was a healthy and wealthy man. He was blameless in God's eyes. One day, the Devil appeared to God in heaven. God pointed out to the Devil how good his servant Job was, but the Devil told God that Job was only good because God had blessed him with so many things. The Devil challenged God and asked for permission to punish Job, thinking that if he punished Job, he would turn and curse God. God allowed the Devil to punish Job, but he forbade him from taking his life. In one day, Job lost everything God had blessed him with. His servants, his livestock, and his ten children all died. That was the first test that the Devil afflicted on Job. The second test the Devil challenged Job in was his health. This time, he was afflicted with terrible skin sores. Although Job was in great misery, he refused to curse God, even though he struggled to accept his circumstances. Job acknowledged the power of God and admitted his limited human knowledge. His response pleased God, so God returned Job's health and blessed him with twice as much as before. (SparkNotes, Editors, 2005) This helped me realize that it doesn't matter how blameless we are, we're always tested in some form. If you remain faithful and trust God, he will remain faithful to you and restore what's been lost. It's not always easy to trust the process, and there were a lot of times when it was a challenge for me to silence my mind from the negative thoughts. I still struggle from time to time, but as I continue to grow through this journey, it's clear that it is worth the fight.

In fact, that is why I love the quote, "God gives his toughest battles to his strongest soldiers." I had often heard that saying, but it never really applied to me that much until I became one of those soldiers facing a tough battle. When you experience a traumatic injury, you have to hold on to faith and have a strong mentally. But having a strong mentally doesn't happen overnight; it's a process. It is in those moments of struggle where you find your strength.

When COVID-19 hit, it made me sink back into that depressive stage that I had fought so hard to come out of. Everybody had to quarantine for a little while, which was depressing for the entire world, but when the quarantine lifted, I was still on lockdown. I simply couldn't risk it with my health condition while the virus was still out there. After a while, things got pretty boring just sitting in the house all day. My appetite had slowed up again, I started having chest pains due to anxiety, and I was constantly overthinking my problems. But God is so good, because this time I was able to pick myself up (with the help of my mom) before it got too far. My mama was there to encourage me with positive affirmations, making me realize that I'm never alone and that the circumstances could have been much worse. So in that moment, I had to learn to be content and continue to focus on better days that lay ahead.

We all face trials in life, whether it be a health issue, financial situation, or something else entirely. As I continue to grow through this journey, I'm learning that it's all about how you respond to these trials when you face them. At the early stages of my injury, my response to everything was negative because I was still clinging to my old life and how I used to live so freely. By me clinging on, I had a fear that I was missing out on everything. I was only twenty-five and having to face the fact that I would never get the time back as long as I was in a wheelchair. I feared I would miss out on living the life I had dreamed of as a young adult, and I even feared that I would become less relevant in the world.

~

AS THE YEARS passed since my injury, I understood that I was in a season that required me to be alone. I had to block out all the noise so I could really get to know myself and get to know more about God. At first, I had the mentality of the world that if I wasn't doing certain things by a certain age, I was behind in life, and the wheelchair was certainly holding me up. What I now realize is that God created time and he has the power to redeem the time I thought I missed out on. Just like things can go bad in a blink of an eye, things can also change tremendously for the better in a blink of an eye, and that right there makes up for all lost time. The Bible states in 2 Peter 3:8, "A day is like a thousand years to the Lord, and a thousand years is like a day." That verse helps remind me that his timing is not our timing, and it's never too late as long as he allows breath in your body.

I named this chapter *The Bigger Picture* because I was crippled by life's circumstances until I finally accepted what had happened to me. I didn't realize that the purpose behind the wait and the pain was that God was transforming me on the inside and out. Through the transformation, God has helped me gain strength, courage, and a newfound confidence both spiritually and physically. I've gained strength in him spiritually by knowing that he's my "refuge and strength, always ready to help in times of trouble." (Psalms 46:1) I've realized that God wants me to let him help me no matter what the circumstances are, and to stop trying to figure it out on my own.

I've gained strength physically in the injury itself by accomplishing goals that I couldn't at first. I can now sit up without falling over, feed myself without assistance, pick up things, write, and the list goes on. I've gained courage by pushing myself and working towards new goals every day by not giving up, even if I don't get it right the first time. I know that eventually God will help me prevail, and I've gained a newfound confidence by sharing my story with people every day on how God has helped me through the darkest moments of my life.

I'm no longer embarrassed by my condition, because I now know that life doesn't have to stop because I'm in this wheelchair. The sky is the limit for me. In the beginning, I kept hoping that things would start functioning immediately, not realizing that the small accomplishments would turn into big accomplishments. Just like a newborn baby learning to crawl before they walk, the best is yet to come. I'll never lose hope that one day I'll do all the things I desire, like walk again, get married, have kids, and even drive again since I was blessed with a vehicle that's wheelchair accessible. It amazes me at the things I find myself accomplishing now, and I know it's all because of God. What keeps me going is my faith in him, confidently knowing that he will give me everything that I desire according to his will.

I often think about that tragic night of the accident and realize how blessed I am that I didn't die at a young age. I am thankful that I didn't become another statistic as a young adult dying in a fatal crash, with alcohol being the root cause. I also think about how if I had died that night, I would have missed out on many opportunities in life, and most importantly, I would have missed out on getting to know God on a personal level. Like I mentioned before, I've always been a church girl, but I didn't pray like I should and I never took the time to read the Bible to learn more about God. I always kept him on standby for when it was convenient for me. Now that he's given me a second chance at life, I spend my time reading the Bible and learning his character. This brings me great joy and reminds me of my purpose in life, which is to spread the good news about how great our Creator is and to encourage many to follow his path by letting him lead the way in every aspect of life. I'm never going to be perfect, but every day I'm a work in progress. Now I look at life from a different perspective, and each morning when I wake up, I thank God for allowing me to see another day. Things can change so fast, and I'm beyond grateful that I still have the chance to live a meaningful life.

Reader,

I wrote this book to be an inspiration to many. I pray that through my story, you will find hope, comfort, joy, and peace in overcoming any challenge that comes your way. You never know what the future holds, but God does. Put your trust in Him. Also, stay humble, prayed up, and be blessed. I would love for you to continue to follow me on my journey through the links below. Thanks for your support.

Facebook: https://www.facebook.com/arci.davis

Instagram: https://www.instagram.com/arcivictoria_/

THEN

NOW